Who Was The Voice From The Fire?

Biblically and Historically Revealing the True Nature of the Angel of God

By Daniel Reidmiller

Copyright © 2025 by Daniel Reidmiller

All rights reserved. No part of this book may be produced
or
distributed in any form without the author's written permission.

First Edition: May 20, 2025

ISBN: 979-8-3493-4574-6

Chapters

1. In the Beginning Was the Word
2. I AM – Yahshua in the Fire
3. The Angel Who Saves – Yahshua in the Old Testament
4. Sin, Silence, and Compromise
5. The Names That Reveal Him – Prophecies of Yahshua as YHWH
6. The Feasts That Foretold Him – Yahshua in the Appointed Times
7. The Blood and the Covenant
8. The Temple, the Veil, and the Body
9. He Is Coming Again
10. The Fire Still Speaks

Preface

I didn't write this book to sound like a theologian or to stack it high with academic arguments. I didn't write it for the purpose of debate or to please a religious crowd with advanced degrees. I wrote it because the truth has already been spoken, and it's time it was presented plainly. This is not a complicated book. It's not designed to be. It is a clear, biblically accurate, historically grounded presentation of who Yahshua Messiah is and always has been, the very Word of YHWH, the Angel of the LORD, the voice from the fire, and the only Savior of mankind.

The Bible is not vague. It is not evolving. It does not change with the times, and it does not leave room for personal revision. Either one follows it, or one doesn't. Either Yahshua is Lord, or He isn't. Either we submit to Scripture, or we place ourselves above it, and in doing so, reject it altogether. A person cannot claim to be a follower of Messiah, a

Christian, and support things that YHWH explicitly calls sin. You cannot support abortion, which is the murder of the innocent, and still claim to walk with the Creator who formed life in the womb. You cannot support gay or trans lifestyles and still call yourself a Christian, because doing so directly opposes YHWH's design for creation and the clear teachings of both the Old and New Testaments.

This book does not make space for compromise. That's not because I'm harsh. It's because YHWH's Word doesn't change, and neither does He. I've written this so that the average person, not the theologian or the academic, can pick it up, read it, and be confronted with truth. Not my truth. Not a church's truth. Just Scripture, presented plainly, with no wriggle room. This book won't sit well with everyone. It's not supposed to. Truth divides. Light exposes darkness. And Yahshua said clearly that He came not to bring peace but a sword.

Chapter 1: In the Beginning Was the Word

Before anything was made—before light, stars, or mankind—there was the Word.

John 1:1–3 tells us:

"In the beginning was the Word, and the Word was with God, and the Word was God. The same was in the beginning with God. All things were made by Him; and without Him was not any thing made that was made."

The Word is Yahshua Messiah, the eternal Son of YHWH. He was not created, not born in eternity, and not an afterthought. He is God, present before time. This truth, often overlooked or buried beneath religious tradition, is plainly spoken in Scripture.

When YHWH created the heavens and the earth in Genesis 1, He spoke. Each time He said "Let there be," something sprang into existence. But that Word wasn't just sound. It was the active presence of Yahshua Messiah—the Word through whom all things were made.

Colossians 1:16–17 confirms:

"For by Him were all things created… and by Him all things consist."

Yahshua was not passive at Creation. He was the one forming, shaping, breathing life. The Word was with YHWH—and was YHWH.

This is not doctrine made by men. It is written plainly and repeatedly in the Scriptures. Yahshua is the visible expression of the invisible Elohim. From the first page of Genesis to the last word of Revelation, He is the center.

In Exodus 3, YHWH reveals His name to Moses at the burning bush:

"And Elohim said unto Moses, I AM THAT I AM: and He said, Thus shalt thou say unto the children of Israel, I AM hath sent me unto you… YHWH… this is my name forever."

The Hebrew letters for YHWH—Yod, Heh, Vav, Heh—are

breath sounds. They form no hard syllables. The name is exhaled and inhaled. Say it softly: YH (inhale), WH (exhale). Every breath you take calls His name. From your first cry to your last sigh, you are proclaiming YHWH.

Genesis 2:7 says:

"YHWH Elohim formed man of the dust of the ground, and breathed into his nostrils the breath of life; and man became a living soul."

Whether people recognize Him or not, their very lungs witness to His name. That's not symbolism. It's truth. Every breath praises YHWH—even if the mind rejects Him.

Many mistakenly believe that Yahshua only arrived at Bethlehem. But He didn't begin in the manger. He always existed.

Micah 5:2 speaks of His birth:

"But thou, Bethlehem… out of thee shall He come forth unto Me that is to be ruler in Israel; whose goings forth have been from of old, from everlasting."

From everlasting—before time. He walked the garden with Adam. He visited Abraham. He stood in the fire with Shadrach, Meshach, and Abednego. And He spoke to Moses from the bush.

Yahshua Messiah is not a New Testament invention. He is the living Word. Always present. Always acting. Always saving.

Throughout the Old Testament, a mysterious figure appears again and again—the Angel of YHWH. But He isn't just delivering messages. He speaks as YHWH, receives worship, forgives sins, and declares covenants. No ordinary angel does this. Created angels do not accept worship or declare themselves divine. This Angel is different.

This Angel is not a separate being from YHWH, nor is He a created messenger. He is the visible manifestation of YHWH—His Word made present before flesh. This is Yahshua Messiah, the same yesterday, today, and forever, revealing YHWH to His people long before He was born in Bethlehem.

In Genesis 16, Hagar sees the Angel of YHWH and calls Him *El Roi*—"the God who sees me." In Genesis 22, the Angel of YHWH stops Abraham from sacrificing Isaac and then says, "By Myself have I sworn, saith YHWH…" In Judges 13, the Angel of YHWH appears to Samson's parents. When He ascends in flame, they fall on their faces and cry out, "We shall surely die, for we have seen God."

This is Yahshua—the visible presence of YHWH before He came in flesh. He is the I AM.

In John 8:58, Yahshua declared, "Before Abraham was, I AM"—not "I was." He didn't claim to be like YHWH. He used the exact name YHWH gave to Moses—and the people understood. They tried to stone Him for blasphemy, but it wasn't blasphemy. It was truth.

Yahshua was declaring:
"I am the one who spoke to Moses from the fire."

As we move through Scripture, we see different names used for

God—names that reveal His character and His relationship with humanity. He is called *El Shaddai*, meaning God Almighty, the One with power to fulfill every promise. He is *El Elyon*, God Most High, exalted above all creation. He is *El Gibbor*, the Mighty God—a prophetic title applied directly to the Messiah, Yahshua. And He is known as *Adonai*, Master and Lord, a name spoken with reverence when uttering the sacred name YHWH aloud was considered too holy.

Each of these names reveals another facet of YHWH's nature, and Yahshua bears them all.

Revelation 19:13 speaks of Yahshua's return:

"And He was clothed with a vesture dipped in blood: and His name is called The Word of God."

The Word is coming back—
not in weakness, but in glory.
He was the voice in the garden.
He was the fire in the bush.
He was the commander of the Lord's armies.

He is the Lamb who was slain.
He is the returning King.
He is Yahshua Messiah—YHWH in visible form.

Chapter 2: I AM – Yahshua in the Fire

In the last chapter, we saw that the Word was present before creation. That Word is Yahshua Messiah—the eternal, living expression of YHWH. Now we look at one of the clearest moments in Scripture where He reveals Himself: the burning bush.

The book of Exodus tells us that the Angel of YHWH appeared to Moses in a flame of fire out of the midst of a bush. A bush burned, but was not consumed. This was no illusion. This was a direct manifestation of the divine—YHWH speaking through His visible presence. When YHWH saw that Moses turned aside to see, Elohim called to him out of the midst of the bush and said, "Moses, Moses." The text clearly connects the appearance of the Angel with the voice of YHWH. They are not separate beings. The Angel is not speaking on YHWH's behalf. He is speaking as YHWH.

YHWH then tells Moses, "Draw not near here. Take your shoes off your feet, for the place where you stand is holy ground." Why was it holy? Not because of the fire. Not because of Moses. But because YHWH was there—manifested through His Messenger, who is Yahshua Messiah. This is not a created angel. This is not a representative being. This is YHWH Himself appearing in a form Moses could comprehend and survive.

When Moses asks for a name to give the Israelites, he receives one of the most mysterious and powerful revelations in all of Scripture: "I AM THAT I AM." In Hebrew, the phrase is "Ehyeh Asher Ehyeh." It means "I will be what I will be." It speaks of self-existence, eternal presence, and unchanging nature. YHWH then tells Moses, "This is My name forever, and this is My memorial to all generations." The name given is YHWH—four letters in Hebrew: Yod, Heh, Vav, Heh. These letters form breath sounds. The name requires no movement of the lips or tongue. It can be spoken only through breathing.

Every human being, from their first cry to their final breath, speaks His name. YHWH. The inhale, the exhale. Whether they acknowledge Him or not, every breath bears witness. This is no poetic metaphor. It is the living design of the Creator Himself. In Genesis, YHWH formed man from the dust and breathed into his nostrils the breath of life. Man became a living soul. That same breath—called "ruach" in Hebrew—means both breath and spirit. Life is not just a biological process. It is a spiritual imprint.

The same I AM who called Moses still speaks today. He speaks through the Word. He speaks through the Spirit. He speaks through the breath He gives. Every breath testifies to His presence. Some curse Him. Some ignore Him. But some still fall on their faces before the fire, as Moses did.

When Yahshua Messiah later walked the earth, He did not avoid this identity. He embraced it. In John chapter 8, Yahshua declared to the religious leaders, "Before Abraham was, I AM." He did not say, "I was." He said, "I AM." He used the exact name YHWH gave to Moses. The people listening understood the claim. They picked up stones to kill Him for what they believed was blasphemy. But Yahshua did not blaspheme. He told the truth.

The one who spoke to Moses from the bush, who declared, "I AM THAT I AM," is the same one who stood in the temple courts and said, "I AM." He is not a created messenger. He is not a servant of YHWH. He is YHWH in visible form—Yahshua Messiah, the Angel of YHWH, the Word, the Breath, the Voice from the Fire.

Chapter 3: The Angel Who Saves – Yahshua in the Old Testament

Throughout the Old Testament, there appears a mysterious figure known as the Angel of YHWH. To the casual reader, this may seem like a high-ranking created being sent to speak on behalf of YHWH. But when we read carefully and take the text at face value, we find that this Angel does not merely speak for YHWH. He speaks as YHWH. He does not carry messages. He exercises divine authority. He receives worship. He swears by His own name. He forgives sin. He judges. And He saves.

This is not an ordinary angel. This is not Gabriel. This is not Michael. This is Yahshua Messiah—the eternal Word of YHWH, appearing visibly before taking on flesh. Salvation did not begin in the New Testament. Yahshua did not only arrive at Bethlehem. He has always been the one who saves.

Isaiah 43:11 says, "I, even I, am YHWH; and beside Me there is no saviour." This statement leaves no room for confusion. If there is only one Savior, and Yahshua is that Savior, then Yahshua is YHWH. This truth is not hidden. It is declared plainly by the prophets and fulfilled in the Gospels. Yahshua did not arrive late in the story. He has always been there, and He has always been the one who saves.

In Genesis 16, the Angel of YHWH finds Hagar in the wilderness. He tells her to return to her mistress and promises, "I will multiply thy seed exceedingly, that it shall not be numbered for multitude." No created angel has the authority to make such a promise. The text makes it clear that this being speaks with the authority of YHWH. In verse 13, Hagar responds by naming the one who spoke to her. She calls Him "El Roi," the God who sees. She does not say she saw a messenger. She says she saw God, and she lived. This was not just an angel. It was the visible presence of YHWH.

In Genesis 22, Abraham is tested. He is told to sacrifice his son Isaac. As Abraham raises the knife, the Angel of YHWH calls out to stop him. In verse 11 and 12, the Angel says, "Lay not thine hand upon the lad... for now I know that thou fearest God." Then in verse 15 through 18, the Angel of YHWH speaks again, saying, "By Myself have I sworn, saith YHWH... in thy seed shall all the nations of the earth be blessed." This is not a representative speaking on YHWH's behalf. The Angel speaks as YHWH and makes an oath in His own name. This is the same promise fulfilled through Yahshua Messiah. The one making the promise is the one who later fulfilled it.

In Exodus 23, YHWH warns Israel that He is sending an Angel before them. He says, "Beware of Him, and obey His voice, provoke Him not; for He will not pardon your transgressions: for My name is in Him." This Angel has the authority to forgive or withhold forgiveness. That is a divine prerogative. And YHWH says His name is in this Angel. That can only refer to Yahshua, the one who bore the name of YHWH and had the authority to forgive sins. This was not a mere heavenly servant. This was the pre-incarnate Messiah.

In Judges 6, the Angel of YHWH appears to Gideon and calls him to deliver Israel. Gideon offers a sacrifice, which the Angel touches with His staff. Fire consumes it, and the Angel vanishes. Gideon then realizes who he has seen. He says, "Alas, O Adonai YHWH! for because I have seen the Angel of YHWH face to face." He believes he will die because he knows he has seen God. YHWH responds, "Peace be unto thee; fear not: thou shalt not die." Again, the Angel and YHWH are revealed as the same being—one who accepts worship, commands sacrifice, and declares peace.

In Judges 13, the Angel of YHWH appears to the parents of Samson. Manoah asks for His name, and the Angel replies, "Why askest thou thus after my name, seeing it is secret?" The Hebrew word translated "secret" is "Pili," which also means "Wonderful." This connects directly to

Isaiah 9:6, where the coming Messiah is called Wonderful, Counselor, El Gibbor, Everlasting Father, and Prince of Peace. The Angel ascends in the flame of the altar, and Manoah and his wife fall on their faces. Manoah says, "We shall surely die, because we have seen God." They understood what many today have forgotten. The Angel of YHWH is not just a servant. He is YHWH.

In Zechariah 3, the prophet sees Joshua the high priest standing before the Angel of YHWH, while Satan stands to accuse him. The Angel rebukes Satan and declares, "YHWH rebuke thee, O Satan; even YHWH that hath chosen Jerusalem rebuke thee." Here, the Angel intercedes and defends the priest. This is exactly what Yahshua Messiah does for us. First John 2:1 says, "If any man sin, we have an advocate with the Father, Yahshua Messiah the righteous." Only one person stands before the throne of YHWH as intercessor. Only one silences the accuser. That one is Yahshua.

It is important to note that not every angel in Scripture is Yahshua. The Hebrew word "malakh" simply means messenger, and there are many created angels who serve YHWH. Gabriel appears with messages. Michael fights battles. Others carry out judgment or protection. But the Angel of YHWH who speaks as YHWH, who forgives sins, who accepts worship, and who establishes covenants is not one of them. This Angel is not a created being. He is not a prophet. He is the visible presence of the invisible Elohim. He is the Word before flesh. He is Yahshua Messiah.

From Genesis to Judges, from the wilderness to the altar, from promises to intercession, the Angel of YHWH appears not to inform but to act. He leads. He rescues. He forgives. He saves. This is not a foreshadowing of the Messiah. It is the Messiah. He was present before Bethlehem. He was active long before the Gospels. He was always the one who saved. He was the voice from the fire. He was the hand that stayed the knife. He was the flame on the altar. And He is the same yesterday, today, and forever.

Chapter 4: Sin, Silence, and Compromise

Sin separates. From the very beginning in Eden, sin introduced separation between humanity and YHWH. It brought death, shame, judgment, and exile. It corrupted what was pure. Today, sin has not changed, but the world has learned to disguise it. What once was called wicked is now called brave. What was shameful is now celebrated. And what is righteous is now labeled as hateful. But Scripture remains unchanged. YHWH has not altered His standard.

Sin is not a sliding scale of morality. People tend to rank sins in order of social offense, saying things like, "At least I'm not a murderer," or "At least I don't cheat on my spouse." But that's not how the Word of YHWH measures sin. James 2:10 says, "For whosoever shall keep the whole law, and yet offend in one point, he is guilty of all." If you sin at all, you are guilty of breaking the entire covenant. The proud gossip is no less guilty than the sexually immoral. The dishonest business owner stands just as condemned as the idol worshiper. Sin is not about how bad it seems in comparison to someone else's. It is about how it violates the holiness of YHWH.

There is one sin, however, that Yahshua described as unforgivable. In Matthew 12:31–32, He says, "All manner of sin and blasphemy shall be forgiven unto men, but the blasphemy against the Holy Spirit shall not be forgiven unto men." This is not some accidental word spoken in ignorance. It is a deliberate, ongoing rejection and mockery of the work of YHWH's Spirit. In context, Yahshua had just healed a demon-possessed man, and the religious leaders accused Him of working by the power of Satan. They had seen the goodness of YHWH with their own eyes and still chose to attribute it to evil. That is blasphemy of the Holy Spirit.

This blasphemy can also happen in more subtle and modern forms. When a person persistently mocks YHWH's design, when they embrace rebellion and call it holy, they are walking dangerously close to this unforgivable line. When a man pretends to be a woman and demands society affirm it, he is not simply making a personal choice. He is mocking the creation of YHWH, who made them male and female. When someone ends their own life willingly, apart from unbearable duress or diminished capacity, they are declaring their judgment superior to YHWH's. They destroy what He has made and reject His authority over life and death. These are not unforgivable sins by default, but they are expressions of a deeper rebellion that, if unrepented, can harden into blasphemy.

Even so, we are not called to hate sinners. Yahshua did not avoid sinners. He ate with tax collectors. He spoke gently to adulterers. He healed the unclean. But He never affirmed sin. He never said it was acceptable. When He forgave the woman caught in adultery, He said, "Go, and sin no more." That is the balance. We must love others without affirming what

YHWH calls evil. Romans 1:32 warns that those who support or take pleasure in others' sin are just as guilty. If you support or celebrate sinful behavior—whether out of politeness, fear, or cultural pressure—you share in the sin. Attending a same-sex wedding may seem like a kind gesture, but it is an act of affirmation, a public witness of approval. That makes the Christian complicit in what Scripture calls sin.

Yet while we must not affirm sin, we are also not called to harass people. It is every believer's duty to speak truth and warn others of sin. Ezekiel 3:18 says, "When I say unto the wicked, Thou shalt surely die, and thou givest him not warning... his blood will I require at thine hand." If you know the truth and stay silent, you become accountable. But Titus 3:10 and 2 Timothy 2:24–25 show us how to act. We are to correct once, perhaps twice. Then we move on. We must not strive. We must not become self-righteous crusaders. The servant of YHWH must be gentle, humble, and patient. We speak the truth, and then we let the Spirit do the work.

That brings up a hard question. What about the man on the street corner shouting at passersby? What about the one standing on a milk crate outside the cathedral yelling that the wicked will burn? Is he wrong? Not necessarily in what he says, because Scripture is clear that the unrepentant will face judgment. But his method may be wrong. Yahshua did not scream at sinners in public squares. He sat with them. He touched them. He looked into their eyes. He told them the truth, and He invited them to repent. The man yelling in the street may believe he is doing YHWH's work, but if he is driving people away from the Gospel with cruelty or pride, then even if his message is technically accurate, he may be sinning in his approach.

We must also look inward. Those who believe in truth must live it. We cannot confront others about sin while hiding our own. Romans 3:23 says, "For all have sinned and come short of the glory of God." That includes you. That includes me. There is no room for pride. We speak truth with humility. We do not water it down. We do not delay it. But we must never speak it as if we are above it.

Many sincere Catholics believe they are serving YHWH with reverence. But sincerity is not the standard. Scripture is. Catholic tradition includes praying to saints, bowing before statues, lighting candles to images, and asking Mary to intercede. Yet the Bible is clear. First Timothy 2:5 says, "There is one God, and one mediator between God and men, the man Yahshua Messiah." No one else intercedes. No one else can be approached in prayer. Yahshua Himself said in John 14:6, "No man cometh unto the Father, but by Me." Even if someone says, "I don't worship the statue, I just honor it," the action still violates Exodus 20:4–5, which commands us not to make or bow down to graven images. YHWH does not accept substitutions. He gave His Son as the only way, and He does not share that role with Mary, the saints, or any human invention.

The message is simple, even if it is hard. We must repent. We must speak truth. We must love others, but not affirm their sin. We must warn without pride, and correct without cruelty. Yahshua's call has never changed. He said, "Repent, for the kingdom of heaven is at hand." That means turn around. Change direction. Stop sinning and start following. And once you know Him, you are not to return to sin. Yahshua said to the forgiven woman, "Go and sin no more." That is still the instruction. He has not changed. His standard has not changed. His love is not permission. His grace is not approval. He is holy. He is the same YHWH who spoke from the fire. And He still calls us to be holy as He is holy.

Chapter 5: The Names That Reveal Him – Prophecies of Yahshua as YHWH

From the beginning, YHWH revealed who He is and what He would do. Through His prophets, He declared the coming of the Messiah not only by action but by name. These names were not generic descriptions or symbolic titles. They were direct revelations of divine identity. They pointed to Yahshua Messiah not as a representative of YHWH but as YHWH Himself in visible form. The names of the Messiah tell us plainly that He is the one who spoke from the fire, who walked with Adam, who led Israel, and who will reign forever.

In Isaiah 9:6, the prophet declared, "For unto us a child is born, unto us a son is given: and the government shall be upon His shoulder: and His name shall be called Wonderful, Counsellor, El Gibbor, Everlasting Father, Prince of Peace." Each name in this prophecy reveals divine authority, eternal nature, and sovereign rule. This is not poetic exaggeration. It is revelation. It tells us that the child who would be born would not merely serve YHWH but would be the visible expression of YHWH Himself.

The Hebrew phrase translated "Wonderful, Counsellor" is "Pele' Yo'etz." Pele' means extraordinary or beyond understanding. Yo'etz means counselor or one who gives divine wisdom. This is not a human advisor. This is a title of deity, one who speaks with the wisdom of heaven. Yahshua did not come as a philosopher. He came as the source of truth. Every word He spoke carried eternal weight because He was and is the Word of YHWH.

The next name in the prophecy is El Gibbor, which means Mighty God. El is the standard Hebrew word for God, and Gibbor means mighty or warrior. The same title is used in Isaiah 10:21 to describe YHWH Himself. There is no mistaking the intent. Isaiah is not saying this child will be like God. He is saying this child is God. Yahshua did not merely reflect the power of YHWH. He was and is El Gibbor in the flesh.

Isaiah also calls Him Avi Ad, meaning Everlasting Father. This phrase does not confuse the Son with the Father as separate persons but affirms the eternal nature shared by both. Avi means father, and Ad means everlasting or eternity. Yahshua is not created. He is not temporary. He is the source of eternal life and the embodiment of the eternal presence of YHWH. He is not a man who became divine. He is divinity that took on flesh.

He is also called Sar Shalom, the Prince of Peace. Sar means ruler or prince. Shalom means peace, but also wholeness, completeness, and restoration. Yahshua did not simply bring temporary calm. He is the one who restores what sin has shattered. He is the one who reconciles man to YHWH. He is the one who will establish peace that cannot be broken.

This same truth appears in Micah 5:2, which says, "But thou, Bethlehem Ephratah, though thou be little among the thousands of Judah, yet out of thee shall He come forth unto Me that is to be ruler in Israel; whose goings forth have been from of old, from everlasting." The one born in Bethlehem is not a new being. He is from everlasting. The Hebrew word used here, olam, means eternal, beyond time. Yahshua's beginning did not happen in Mary's womb. He stepped into time, but He existed before it. He was born in Bethlehem, but He did not begin there.

In Isaiah 7:14, the prophet says, "Behold, a virgin shall conceive, and bear a son, and shall call His name Immanuel." This name means God with us. Not a messenger from God. Not a servant of God. Not a prophet pointing to God. God Himself with us. Matthew 1:23 affirms this, stating, "They shall call His name Emmanuel, which being interpreted is, God with us." There is no ambiguity. Yahshua is the fulfillment of this name. He is YHWH in the flesh, dwelling among His people.

Daniel 7:13–14 presents a vision of one like the Son of Man

coming with the clouds of heaven, who is given dominion, glory, and a kingdom that will never pass away. This figure is worshipped by all peoples, nations, and languages. In Hebrew thought, worship belongs only to YHWH. Yet here we see a figure receiving worship and eternal rule. Yahshua constantly referred to Himself as the Son of Man, identifying with this exact prophetic vision. He came once in humility, but He will return in power, fulfilling this vision completely.

The title Son of God has often been misunderstood. Some assume it means Yahshua is lesser than YHWH. But in Hebrew understanding, to be the son of something meant to carry its nature. A son of peace is peaceful. A son of Belial is wicked. The Son of God carries the divine nature of YHWH. John 5:18 explains that the religious leaders sought to kill Yahshua not just for healing on the Sabbath but because He said God was His Father, making Himself equal with God. They understood the claim. Yahshua did not deny it. Instead, He affirmed it, saying in John 14:9, "He that hath seen Me hath seen the Father." He was not claiming to replace the Father, but to perfectly reveal Him. Yahshua is not an ambassador. He is the exact image of YHWH in visible form.

Colossians 1:15 says Yahshua is the image of the invisible God. Hebrews 1:3 says He is the express image of His person. These are not metaphors. These are doctrinal facts. Yahshua reveals what cannot be seen. He makes known what is eternal. Every title, every prophecy, every name points to this truth. He is not one of many. He is not a created being sent by YHWH. He is YHWH.

The name Yahshua itself means YHWH is salvation. This is not coincidence. This is identity. When the angel instructed Joseph to name the child Yahshua, he said, "For He shall save His people from their sins." Salvation does not come from anyone else. There is no other name under heaven given among men by which we must be saved.

The voice that spoke from the bush, the cloud that led through the wilderness, the fire that fell from heaven, and the glory that filled the temple are all expressions of the same being. Yahshua Messiah is not part of the story. He is the story. The names given in prophecy were not guesses. They were declarations. The child born in Bethlehem was El Gibbor. The one who walked among us was Immanuel. The one who died and rose again was the Everlasting Father. And the one who will return is the Prince of Peace. He was named before He was born. He was declared before He appeared. And He is the same YHWH, now and forever.

Chapter 6: The Feasts That Foretold Him – Yahshua in the Appointed Times

In Leviticus chapter 23, YHWH gave seven appointed times to the children of Israel. These were not merely religious festivals. They were rehearsals, prophetic appointments set in motion by YHWH Himself. He called them His feasts. They were never called Jewish holidays in the Scriptures. YHWH said plainly, "These are My feasts." These appointed times, called mo'edim in Hebrew, were designed to point forward to the work of Yahshua Messiah. They reveal His mission, His timing, His death, resurrection, and His return. They are not shadows of things past. They are shadows of Him.

Four of the feasts are fulfilled already in Yahshua's first coming. The remaining three point toward His return. They are perfectly placed in the calendar and in prophetic history. When Yahshua came the first time, He fulfilled the spring feasts. When He returns, He will fulfill the fall feasts. Nothing YHWH does is random. Every word, every sign, every date was set by Him from the beginning.

The first of these is Passover. It remembers the night when the Israelites were spared by the blood of the lamb. Each household that obeyed YHWH's instruction and marked their doorposts with the blood was protected from death. Yahshua was crucified on Passover. He was called the Lamb of God who takes away the sin of the world. Paul says plainly in First Corinthians 5:7 that Yahshua is our Passover. His blood now marks the doors of our hearts, protecting us from the second death. He died at the very hour lambs were being slaughtered in the Temple. This was no accident. It was the fulfillment of the appointed time.

The second feast is Unleavened Bread. For seven days, the Israelites were to eat bread without yeast, a symbol of sin. The feast begins the day after Passover. Yahshua, sinless and without corruption, was placed in the tomb during this feast. His body, like unleavened bread, was pure and unspoiled. In John chapter 6, He called Himself the bread from heaven. His burial during the Feast of Unleavened Bread shows that even in death, He remained without sin. No decay touched Him. His body was not abandoned to corruption.

The third feast is Firstfruits. It occurs the day after the Sabbath following Passover. It was the time when the first sheaf of the barley harvest was waved before YHWH as a promise of the full harvest to come. Yahshua rose from the dead on Firstfruits. Paul calls Him the Firstfruits of those who have fallen asleep. His resurrection is not just a miracle. It is the guarantee of ours. He is the first to rise never to die again. Because He lives, we shall live also.

Fifty days after Firstfruits comes Shavuot, known in Greek as Pentecost, the Feast of Weeks. It celebrates the giving of the Torah at Mount Sinai, when YHWH came down in fire and smoke and gave His covenant to the people. In Acts chapter 2, we see this feast fulfilled again. The Spirit of YHWH came down not in smoke, but in tongues of fire, and wrote His law not on stone but on hearts. The disciples, gathered in obedience during the appointed time, received the power of the Ruach HaKodesh, just as Yahshua promised. The new covenant was not introduced by accident or coincidence. It arrived at the appointed time.

Yahshua fulfilled these four spring feasts with precision. He died on Passover, was buried during Unleavened Bread, rose on Firstfruits, and sent the Spirit on Shavuot. These are historical facts. Their fulfillment is exact. That leaves three feasts remaining. These feasts point forward to what He has not yet done but surely will.

The first of the fall feasts is Yom Teruah, often called the Feast of Trumpets. It is a day of blowing the shofar, a day of awakening, of alarm, and of preparation. There is no historical fulfillment of this feast in Yahshua's first coming. But we are told that He will return with the sound of a trumpet. First Thessalonians 4:16 says the Lord Himself shall descend with a shout and with the trumpet of God. Matthew 24 says He will send His angels with the great sound of a trumpet, and they will gather His elect. The trumpet feast points to His return. The day and hour no man knows, but the sound will announce the arrival of the King.

Next comes Yom Kippur, the Day of Atonement. It is the holiest day on the biblical calendar, a time of affliction, repentance, and national intercession. The high priest entered the Most Holy Place to make atonement for the people. Yahshua has already made atonement with His blood, but this day points forward to the moment when the nation of Israel will see the one whom they pierced and mourn for Him as for a firstborn. Zechariah 12:10 describes that moment. Paul says in Romans 11 that all Israel shall be saved. The Day of Atonement will be fulfilled when the remaining remnant turns to their Messiah and receives Him in repentance and faith.

The final appointed feast is Sukkot, the Feast of Tabernacles. It remembers the time when YHWH dwelt with His people in the wilderness. The people lived in booths, temporary shelters, and celebrated YHWH's provision. This feast points forward to the day when Yahshua will once again dwell among us. Revelation 21:3 says, "Behold, the tabernacle of God is with men, and He will dwell with them." When Yahshua returns to rule and reign, this feast will be fulfilled. Zechariah 14 speaks of a future time when all nations will go up to Jerusalem to worship the King and to keep the Feast of Tabernacles.

Each of these seven appointments speaks of Yahshua. He did not abolish them. He fulfilled them. Paul writes in Colossians 2:17 that the feasts are a shadow of things to come, but the body is of Messiah. The shadow only exists because of the substance. Yahshua is that substance. These feasts are not burdens. They are blueprints. They are not outdated traditions. They are divine prophecy.

YHWH does not act by chance. He declares the end from the beginning. He set the calendar in place long before the cross, and Yahshua walked it out exactly as foretold. He is the Passover Lamb. He is the sinless bread. He is the Firstfruits of resurrection. He is the giver of the Spirit. He is the trumpet blast. He is the returning High Priest. He is the tabernacle that will never be removed.

The voice that spoke from the fire set these appointments in motion. The Word who became flesh fulfilled them. And the King who is coming again will complete the rest. The feasts of YHWH are not relics of the past. They are the map of redemption. And every step of it points to Yahshua Messiah.

Chapter 7: The Blood and the Covenant

The story of YHWH's people has always been a covenant story. It began with a promise to Abraham, was sealed at Mount Sinai with blood, and was fulfilled by Yahshua Messiah at Calvary. The word covenant is often misunderstood today. It is not a casual agreement or a flexible arrangement. In Hebrew, it is a binding oath, a permanent relationship, often sealed in blood. It means life and death. In Exodus chapter 24, we see YHWH establish His covenant with Israel. Moses reads the words of the law to the people, and they respond, "All that YHWH hath said we will do, and be obedient." Then Moses builds an altar and offers sacrifices. He takes the blood, sprinkles half on the altar, and the other half on the people. He says, "Behold the blood of the covenant, which YHWH hath made with you." That blood sealed the covenant. It confirmed the bond between YHWH and Israel. It was not a suggestion. It was a life-and-death agreement.

But there was a problem. The people could not keep the covenant. Despite their vows, they sinned again and again. The blood of bulls and goats could cover sin temporarily, but it could not cleanse the conscience. It could not make a man truly holy. The sacrifices had to be repeated year after year. The high priest could only enter the Holy of Holies once a year, and even then, not without blood. Hebrews chapter 10 tells us that the law was a shadow of good things to come, but not the very image. It could not make the worshipers perfect. If it could, the sacrifices would have ceased. But they didn't. The blood of animals was not enough.

That is why Yahshua came. At the Last Supper, as He shared the cup with His disciples, He said, "This is My blood of the new covenant, which is shed for many for the remission of sins." He was not quoting tradition. He was fulfilling prophecy. Jeremiah 31 had foretold a new covenant, one not written on stone but on hearts.

Yahshua declared that the covenant was no longer sealed with the blood of lambs, but with His own blood. He became the Lamb. He was both priest and sacrifice. His blood was not sprinkled on an altar of stone but poured out on a cross. And He did not enter an earthly tabernacle, but the heavenly one. Hebrews 9 says He entered once into the holy place, having obtained eternal redemption for us.

The blood of Yahshua is not symbolic. It is real, and it is the foundation of everything we believe. Without it, there is no forgiveness. Without it, there is no access to YHWH. Without it, the covenant would remain broken. But with it, the veil is torn, the way is open, and the curse of sin is destroyed. The covenant at Sinai was mediated through Moses. The new covenant is mediated through Yahshua. The first covenant was conditional and fragile. The new covenant is eternal and unbreakable. Yahshua said in John 6, "Except ye eat the flesh of the Son of man, and drink His blood, ye have no life in you." This was not a call to ritual. It was a call to covenant. To be in covenant with Him is to partake of His life and surrender to His rule.

Blood is not a metaphor. It is the cost of sin. From the garden of Eden, where animals were slain to cover Adam and Eve's nakedness, to the sacrifices of the tabernacle, to the hill of Golgotha, the message is the same. Sin brings death. Only blood brings atonement. Leviticus 17:11 says, "The life of the flesh is in the blood, and I have given it to you upon the altar to make an atonement for your souls." Yahshua did not come to remove this truth. He came to fulfill it. He laid down His life and poured out His blood. It was not taken from Him. He gave it freely.

When He died, the veil in the temple was torn from top to bottom. That was not just a sign of mourning. It was a declaration. The barrier between YHWH and man was removed. The way into the Most Holy Place was opened, not by human hands, but by the torn flesh of the Son of God. The covenant was sealed, not in ritual, but in reality. The cross was not a symbol of defeat. It was the altar of victory.

Today, many try to come to YHWH through other means. Some trust in tradition. Others trust in good works. But the covenant is only entered through the blood of Yahshua. There is no other way. Hebrews 10:29 warns that those who despise the blood of the covenant insult the Spirit of grace. This is not a small matter. The blood of Yahshua is holy. It is precious. It is the only means by which we are cleansed. We cannot mix it with human effort. We cannot improve it with ceremony. It is complete and sufficient.

The covenant calls for response. It is not passive. It demands faith, obedience, and surrender. Just as the people of Israel stood before the mountain and said, "We will obey," so we too must declare our allegiance. But unlike them, we are not left to our own strength. The same Spirit who raised Yahshua from the dead now lives in those who believe. He writes the law on our hearts. He enables us to walk in holiness. The covenant is not just an agreement. It is a transformation.

The voice that spoke from the fire made a covenant with His people. The Word made flesh sealed that covenant with His own blood. The same YHWH who spoke at Sinai now speaks through His Son. And the call remains: come into covenant with Me. Receive the blood. Walk in obedience. Live in My presence. The covenant is not canceled. It is fulfilled. And it is eternal.

Chapter 8: The Temple, the Veil, and the Body

From the time of Moses, YHWH instructed His people to build Him a dwelling place. The tabernacle was crafted according to heavenly patterns, not human imagination. Every curtain, measurement, and vessel was designed to point to something greater. When the tabernacle was complete, YHWH's presence filled it. Later, Solomon's Temple became the permanent home for the Ark of the Covenant. In both cases, the center of it all was the Most Holy Place, where the presence of YHWH dwelled above the mercy seat. No one could enter that space except the high priest, and only once a year on the Day of Atonement, and never without blood.

The separation between YHWH and man was marked by a veil. This was not a thin curtain. It was thick, woven, and massive, symbolizing the barrier that sin placed between humanity and holiness. To approach the Most High without cleansing was to die. The people of Israel knew the temple was sacred because YHWH's presence was not casual. It was terrifying in its purity. The sacrifices offered daily in the outer courts reminded the people that sin was costly and that access to YHWH was restricted. Priests had to be set apart. Rituals had to be followed. Nothing could be improvised.

Yet this system was never the goal. It was a shadow of what was coming. Hebrews tells us that the law, the priesthood, and the temple were copies of the heavenly things. They were never the destination. They were the signs pointing to it. Yahshua spoke openly about the temple. When He overturned the tables of the moneychangers, He declared it had become a den of thieves. When He was challenged, He said, "Destroy this temple, and in three days I will raise it up." The people were confused, thinking He referred to the stone structure. But He was speaking of His body.

Yahshua referred to Himself as the temple because He is the dwelling place of YHWH in human form. Colossians 2:9 says, "For in Him dwelleth all the fullness of the Godhead bodily." He was not a prophet pointing to the presence. He was the presence. In Him, YHWH walked among His people again, not in smoke or fire, but in flesh. His body was the tabernacle. His words were the voice from within. His blood was the offering. And His death would open the way.

When Yahshua died, the veil in the temple was torn in two from top to bottom. That detail matters. It was not torn by man from the ground up. It was torn by YHWH from above, as a sign that the barrier was removed. The Holy of Holies was no longer off-limits. The way into the presence of YHWH was now open, not to a select priesthood, but to all who come through Yahshua. The veil had served its purpose. The body of Yahshua, pierced and broken, became the new and living way.

Hebrews 10:19–20 says, "Having therefore, brethren, boldness to enter into the holiest by the blood of Yahshua, by a new and living way, which He hath consecrated for us, through the veil, that is to say, His flesh." This is the heart of the Gospel. The temple was never about bricks or gold. It was always about access. And Yahshua has given us that access. He is the High Priest. He is the Sacrifice. He is the Mercy Seat. And He is the Veil that was torn.

The temple also pointed to the gathering of the redeemed. Paul writes in First Corinthians 3:16, "Know ye not that ye are the temple of God, and that the Spirit of God dwelleth in you?" Through Yahshua, the people of YHWH become the temple. His Spirit no longer dwells in a room but in His people. The priesthood is not abolished but fulfilled. We are now a royal priesthood, a holy nation, a people for His own possession.

The destruction of the Second Temple in 70 AD did not end worship. It confirmed what Yahshua had already declared. The time had come when true worshipers would worship the Father in spirit and in truth, not on a mountain or in a building, but in the heart. The old system, with its external forms, gave way to the living reality of Yahshua's presence among and within His people.

This truth does not make the old system worthless. It makes it fulfilled. Every lamb slain, every priestly robe, every drop of oil, and every trumpet blast had meaning. But now the reality has come. To return to the shadow is to ignore the light. Yahshua is the temple because He is the place where man and YHWH meet. He is the veil because He is the only way in. He is the offering because only His blood cleanses. And He is the High Priest because only He can intercede forever.

The voice that spoke from the fire did not remain distant. He drew near. He entered His temple. He became flesh and tabernacled among us. And when He was raised, He did not abandon us. He sent His Spirit to dwell within us, making our bodies

His temple. The fire did not go out. It moved inside.

Chapter 9: He Is Coming Again

From the beginning, the Word of YHWH has moved forward with purpose. Yahshua Messiah did not come to start something. He came to fulfill what had been written and to finish what had been promised. Yet His first coming was not the end of the story. The prophets, the apostles, and Yahshua Himself all pointed to a day still to come. That day is not symbolic. It is not metaphorical. It is a real day, on a real calendar, when the King will return in glory. The voice that once spoke from the fire and later walked among men will speak again, this time with the sound of a trumpet and the command of a King.

The return of Yahshua is not an add-on to the Gospel. It is the culmination. Without His return, there is no justice. Without His return, the promises remain incomplete. Yahshua spoke plainly about His second coming. In Matthew 24, He described signs in the heavens, distress among nations, and false prophets deceiving many. He warned His disciples not to be misled. He said the coming of the Son of Man would be like lightning flashing across the sky, unmistakable and sudden. He did not say it would be hidden. He said every eye would see it.

The apostles confirmed this. In Acts chapter 1, after Yahshua ascended, two messengers stood by and told the disciples that He would return in the same way they saw Him go. He went up visibly. He will return visibly. In First Thessalonians 4, Paul writes that the Lord Himself will descend from heaven with a shout, with the voice of the archangel, and with the trumpet of God. The dead in Messiah will rise first. Then those who are alive and remain will be caught up to meet Him. This is not poetic language. It is the clear expectation of the early believers.

Revelation gives us a fuller picture. Chapter 19 describes a rider on a white horse, called Faithful and True. His eyes are like fire. On His head are many crowns. He is clothed in a robe dipped in blood, and His name is called the Word of God. Out of His mouth comes a sharp sword. He strikes the nations and rules with a rod of iron. This is not the humble teacher of Galilee. This is the conquering King, returning to judge and to reign. His title is King of Kings and Lord of Lords.

The world today has tried to make Yahshua into a soft figure, tolerant of all sin, unconcerned with righteousness. But the Scriptures declare otherwise. He is merciful, but He is also just. He is patient, but He is also holy. His second coming will not be as a lamb, but as a lion. He will not be mocked. He will not be ignored. The nations will mourn when they see Him, because they will know the truth they rejected is now undeniable.

This return is also the hope of the righteous. For those who belong to Him, His coming is not a terror but a triumph. It is the day when justice is restored, when tears are wiped away, when suffering ends and righteousness reigns. Paul called it the blessed hope, the glorious appearing of our great

God and Savior, Yahshua Messiah. The early believers lived in expectation of that day. They faced persecution, death, and exile with the firm conviction that the King was coming back. That hope gave them courage. It should give us the same.

There will be signs before His return. Yahshua said there would be wars and rumors of wars, famines, pestilence, and earthquakes in various places. He said lawlessness would increase, and the love of many would grow cold. He said the Gospel would be preached to all nations, and then the end would come. These are not predictions we are free to ignore. They are warnings to stay awake, to remain faithful, to keep our lamps burning.

No one knows the day or the hour, but we are not to live in darkness. We are children of light. We are to discern the times and live in readiness. That means living in holiness, preaching the truth, rejecting compromise, and enduring hardship. The return of Yahshua is not just a hope. It is a call to action. It is a reminder that we will give an account.

That every hidden thing will be revealed. That every knee will bow, and every tongue will confess that Yahshua Messiah is Master, to the glory of YHWH the Father.

The one who came as a servant will return as a sovereign. The one who died in weakness will return in power. The one who was pierced will return with fire in His eyes. The one who rose from the grave will return to raise the dead and judge the living. The same voice that spoke from the fire, that called to Moses, that walked among fishermen and tax collectors, will speak again. And when He does, the heavens and the earth will shake.

Chapter 10: The Fire Still Speaks

From Genesis to Revelation, YHWH has never been silent. He spoke creation into existence. He spoke to Noah, to Abraham, to Moses from the midst of fire. He spoke through prophets, through storms, through whispers, and ultimately through His Son, Yahshua Messiah. He has never left mankind without witness. He has never withdrawn His voice from those willing to hear. And though the Temple is gone, the Ark of the Covenant hidden, the bush no longer burns on Sinai, the fire still speaks.

The Word of YHWH is not past tense. It is living and active, sharper than any two-edged sword. It still convicts. It still reveals. It still judges the thoughts and intents of the heart. Yahshua is still the Word made flesh. His Spirit still testifies to the truth. He still calls the broken, confronts the rebellious, comforts the faithful, and warns the stubborn. He is not silent. It is the world that has stopped listening.

In days past, YHWH spoke through signs and wonders. He split seas, rained fire from heaven, and raised the dead. Today, many ask why He no longer does these things. The answer is not that He has changed, but that the world has hardened. In Matthew 12, Yahshua said that a wicked generation seeks a sign, but none would be given except the sign of Jonah. That sign was resurrection, and that sign has already been given. The tomb is empty. The King is alive. He has nothing to prove. Now the question is not whether He still speaks, but whether we still hear.

The modern church has grown quiet where it should speak, and loud where it should be silent. It has traded holiness for popularity, doctrine for entertainment, and reverence for relevance. The fire that once burned with conviction now flickers behind stage lights and marketing campaigns. But YHWH does not change. The same fire that fell on Mount Carmel, the same fire that lit the bush and filled the Temple, still waits for hearts prepared in obedience.

For those who seek Him in truth, the fire still speaks. It burns away compromise. It purifies motives. It drives out fear. It does not entertain. It consumes. The Spirit of YHWH is not tame. He is not a mood or a feeling or a background presence. He is holy. He is powerful. He is the same Spirit who raised Yahshua from the dead, and He dwells in those who belong to Him. That fire is not symbolic. It is the presence of the Living God.

Scripture tells us that YHWH is a consuming fire. This is not poetic flourish. It is divine warning. His presence demands holiness. His Word demands obedience. His Spirit demands surrender. Too often, believers ask for the fire of YHWH without preparing the altar. They ask for His power without offering their lives. They want His blessing without repentance. But there is no shortcut to presence. There is no access without blood. There is no fire without sacrifice.

Yahshua still calls His people to carry His cross, not just admire it. He still says, "Follow Me," not "Watch Me." The fire still speaks, not in confusion or ambiguity, but in power and clarity. It speaks through Scripture. It speaks through conviction. It speaks through the still small voice that cuts deeper than any shout. It calls the prodigal home. It calls the lukewarm to repent. It calls the righteous to stand firm. It calls the faithful to endure. It speaks to the humble, but it burns against the proud.

The world grows darker by the day. Evil is called good. Children are taught to curse their Creator. Truth is treated as hate. And still, the fire speaks. It speaks judgment over rebellion. It speaks mercy over repentance. It speaks hope to the faithful remnant who have not bowed to the idols of culture or convenience. The fire speaks to those who listen. And it will speak again in finality, when the heavens roll back, and the Son of Man returns in power.

Until then, the voice from the fire is calling. Not to religion. Not to performance. But to covenant. To holiness. To surrender. To truth. The same voice that called Moses now calls through Yahshua. The same presence that filled the Temple now fills His people. The same fire that burned on Sinai now burns in the hearts of those who refuse to compromise. That fire is not gone. It is not silent. It still speaks. And it is calling His people to be holy, for He is holy.

www.ingramcontent.com/pod-product-compliance
Lightning Source LLC
LaVergne TN
LVHW052004060526
838201LV00059B/3828